# Never-Ne

Written by
Stephen Rickard

Illustrated by
Andy Hamilton

Ransom

This is Never-Never Nick.

Never-Never Nick has a cat, Buzz.

Can you see Buzz?

Never-Never Nick will never visit a shop.

He waits for his shopping to turn up in a van.

Never-Never Nick will never cook his supper.

He gets his fish and chips in a box.

Never-Never Nick will never sing a song.

He has such fear, for he cannot sing!

Never-Never Nick will
never surf in the summer.

He might get his feet wet!

Never-Never Nick chills in the hot sun, but he never has much fun.

He will never sail in a boat.

He will never look for shells.

Never-Never Nick will never bash a nail with a hammer.

He might get hurt!

Can Never-Never Nick fix things?

No! He keeps all his tools in his tool shed.

Never-Never Nick never has fun.

But his cat, Buzz, has too much fun!

Go, Buzz, go!